Head Tilted

A Collection of Poems

Mandy Brincatt

Head Tilted – A Collection of Poems

Author: Mandy Brincatt

Copyright © 2024 Mandy Brincatt

The right of Mandy Brincatt to be identified as author of this work has been asserted by the author in accordance with section 77 and 78 of the Copyright, Designs and Patents Act 1988.

ISBN 978-1-83538-230-1 (Paperback)
978-1-83538-231-8 (E-Book)

Cover Illustration by: Laurel Molly

Cover Design and Book Layout by:
White Magic Studios
www.whitemagicstudios.co.uk

Published by:
Maple Publishers
Fairbourne Drive, Atterbury,
Milton Keynes,
MK10 9RG, UK
www.maplepublishers.com

A CIP catalogue record for this title is available from the British Library.

All rights reserved. No part of this book may be reproduced or translated by any form or by any means, electronic or mechanical, including photocopying, recording or by any information storage and retrieval system without written permission from the author.

This book is a memoir. It reflects the author's recollections of experiences over time. Some names and characteristics have been changed, some events have been compressed, and some dialogues have been recreated, and the Publisher hereby disclaims any responsibility for them.

This book is dedicated to my lovely little family,
John and Will.
When I'm happy, I write, and you make me the happiest of all.

Contents

Gentle Beginnings

A Touch Goodbye	8
After Life	9
Afterthought	10
Depth	11
Deserted	12
Edelweiss	13
Eventually Dust	15
Final Look	16
Fledglings	17
For R.S. Thomas	18
Glass Rose	19
Head Tilted	20
Little Pink Nose	21
Moonshine	22
Poet Tree	24
Safe With Me	25
School of Thought	27
Strait-lace	28
The Gift	29
The Mistake	30
Tilled Earth	31
Traditional Murderer	32
Undisturbed	33
Victory Song	34
Windows	35
Your Eyes	36

Midway Point

Absence	38
Acts	39
Balloons	41
Ceramic	42
Cross-stitches	44
Desir de l'Ange	45
Favourite Sitting	46
Hope	47
How It Must Be	48
I Wish	49
J Shed	50
Life in a Cemetery	51
Meaning	52
November	53
Quiet	54
Salisbury Eve	55
Tealight	56
Thirty-one	57
Thistle and Twilight	58
Tresses	60
Vienna to London 1936	61
Words	62
You Took Flight	63

The Other Day

1853 - 1890	66
1926 - 1962	67
Best. Day. Ever.	68
BFF	69
Clove Hitch Knot	71
Gwendraeth	72
In a Marriage	73
Labour of Love	74
Like it's 1998	75
Mother, How Was I Made?	76
NY	77
Oestrogen	78
Peeling Mushrooms	79
Positive	80
Stella	81
The Poetess' Husband	82
The Same	83
Trolls	84
Unexpected Visitor	85
We Dared to Dance in Odeon	86
You Are Here	87

Gentle Beginnings

A Touch Goodbye

Tears of long held breath
blind to sharing our gift,
my voice quietens to a hush
as you sleep and shift

into lost meadows of dreams,
restless as a child's honey-eye
focusing on intrigue
and chasing blue butterflies.

Grasping your hand to return
from that enchanting boundary,
wrinkles lace your lily skin
as pale as I am lonely.

White roses marry into the night
catching your Gypsy necklace,
an old smile creeps upon your face,
excited and reckless

as you once were in flower fields,
open to the pages of care
and dandelion seeds brushed
through your black-shine hair,

but now you are unsurprised
as cherished candles force
a silent prayer around your room,
their wicks bend in remorse.

*

Instead of stroking
the wet lids of your eyes,
I gave your cold shadow
a warm touch goodbye.

After Life

Delicate death
forever closed and smokey
as black satin tulip, a keyhole.

My life holds
the key, not asking
I tread the first step to reveal

unnatural colours,
familiar faces. Blurring
into myself, becoming part of what I see.

No somber notes.
There is trespassing quiet
and freedom mellows the solitude.

Angels' breaths
blow sweet confusion,
immortality seals an endless tryst

within unchanged surroundings
in white worship
of mist.

Afterthought

The cart upturned
Heavy wood is split

Round and round
The wheel is turning

Placid, merciful
The rain falls

Morning is patient
Corpse faces down

His damp carnation
Matted in the clay

A taste in the air
Of fate

Breath stolen by the wind
Dead fingers plead

With overlapping roots
Around the corner

Bells chime
Eyes still wide open

Shocked and lifeless
The trees pray.

Depth

Murky mirrors distort beneath you,
look at you,
stare at you.
Pay enough attention
and it's your features scraped across the face,
drowning your spirit, your grace.

In rain
ever-increasing circles glide to the edge,
mimicking a looking glass.
Trees lean to peer at themselves,
branches strain to touch their reflections.
Bending to its will.

The surface is calm and inviting.
How far down does it go?
Could you lose yourself?
Would you blend with the scenery?
A hostage in the image
of the puddle.

Everything upside down and distorted,
confusing and not right
and you yearn to be on firm ground again.
To be on the outside.

Deserted

The creeping sea comes
    closer to his other half
  the sand of soft option
she is tranquil powder
    submissive under his blue eyes
      she ebbs away like shy clouds
        rushing past to conceal
  he tries to mould her
into muddy sculptures
  tries to hold her
    glimpses of fresh skin
    but it is impossible to listen
he has no words only reason
  and she waits to know his answer
      in vain.

  They lose
    their love in strokes of struggle
his waves retreat
  leaving only scars and shells
    land is abandoned
      her bosom filled with butterflies
  she awaits night for comfort
but he returns as promised
    like a sacrifice needing an answer
      eyes of angry dust in a twisting end
  she becomes as soundless as the tide
    and brings him pain.

Edelweiss

like a spider unfastened
despite the web
the same feeling
harbours a small handful
of insights
like a coin leaving a pattern
in the palm of a hand
pressed into the shape
of trust
offered to an innocent
with a sweet smile
evacuating any contemplation
of a trick
perhaps

a needful fortune
sharpening the rim
of our senses
a truth straying
at the white edges of day
spreading to a meagre window
with no protection
only split frames
and a poverty of smiles
thrown into the embers
purring in the fireplace
near where this lady sits
reading

her globe by candlelight
a glass future
an ally
Edelweiss soothes the scent
of distrust
when in a single breath
she could find me approaching

her candescent mind
one white flower
hangs in shame from my fingers
like poison trembling
in the breeze
after the door to salvation
is shut

I wait in shade
swathed in hushed air
until she darts
doubt into my stare
finding no place
in homely words
overspilling her chant like a child
the sun doesn't whiten her features
it relaxes her hands
crouching over her instrument
staying true
to its guiding answer
its pulse

flaying my decisions
they dispel into mesmerising smoke
the candle is a clock
a witness to all I hold close
like the coin in my hand
and the life I had planned
but for the realisation
of a truth
that all time can be given
with the same gentle gesture
as the same closed eyes
that deny it

Eventually Dust

She stares from inside,
embracing the change. Outwardly
subtly folding back her crimpled
copper leaves
tightly
un-
forgiving her thoughts.
Surrounded in fog, listening
closely to the past, she spreads frost
along her golden skin. Brushing
the patterned, frayed shapes
too soon. Piercing
deep regret
against
night
air.
Turning
her back to the field
and destroying herself. Her
falling hunger runs like famine,
curdling as it's met by a long-forgotten
wind, forcing each leaf to curl
with shame. Until she is
left pure
silver
in dust.

Final Look

Life
    a comma in the middle,
time
    a full-stopping riddle,
spelling
    is curled, twisting page
mistakes
    increasing, increasing rage.
Waiting
    trying to submerge in lies,
reality
    difficult, sense disguised.
Spinning
    endlessly till cracked,
stepping
    forward, two steps back.
Fading
    like melting to distance,
knotted
    in breath a resistance.
Last
    thought is understood,
very
    last nail in damp wood.
Knock
    all is revealed inside,
people
    in death, cannot hide.

Fledglings

Tiny swallows brooded and protected
safe under a mother's heat,
sleeping under wing,
a tug on strings.
Never wanting to leave
the familiar.
Quickly growing
responsibilities.
Preening feathers,
beginning to rehearse
their limbs.
Peeping at the horizon
from behind the curtain,
imagining their vast possibilities.
Eager wings are rolled
like tight scrolls

- one tug at the ribbon
and they fan out with new strength. They leap into the spotlight.
The swallows' first flight is a graceful, sustained, winning performance.
Bowing and flourishing. Ready to face ....

For R.S. Thomas

Like a grain of dust
Perfect for a moment
Brushing against the cheeks
Of paced winds of time
Unchanging while tracing the lines
Of an old face
His destiny lost in Valleys
Weakening the bones as heavy as sand
And eager fingers touch to slow
As dusk sketches the stormy trees
In confession
Far above his hill
The open air coughs
And a silky chill cradles
Yawning snowdrops, stretching fields
In Celtic mist
Laying its breath in the distance
And causing eyes to shut
Like curtains
While night pours a rhythm
Of sigh-like words
And the creamy moon
Cannot influence haunted stones
And rooted company in rooms
Spinning tales across slate
And lighting empty stools
Behind a door of vast memories
Washed clean by pride
While mirrored glances
And chasing voices
Drift by the windows
Of a world
Too sacred to enter by foot

Glass Rose

So mint-pale and young,
slumbering naive inside,
so plump, so ripe
ready to awaken.

Unfolding like a treasured book,
so frail the plush sheets
sheltered in warmth,
so soft to the print of a thumb.

So unmistakable a scent
like an opera being breathed in,
robbing the senses,
so heady with notes.

But then.

Crystal rain
plummets
splintering the unprepared petals,
encasing them tight.
Frost-bitten lips, pursing the tips,
tragic glass.
Somberly divine.

Head Tilted

Precious beacons
shimmering.
Pinpricks of beauty
unmatched.
Serenely obedient
clasped in a pattern.
Endearing
pepper-shaking
across the night.

Head tilted grounded.
Well-built
wondering.
Doe-eyed
mastering soft contact
and gazing up
sanguinely.
Declining to touch.
Seeming close
yet spoken for.

Little Pink Nose

Black bubbled blackberries,
a hanging vine of plump grapes.
Tiny paws hold tight the fancy fruit.
Little pink nose twitches
and thin whiskers dance,
feet squidge in furry moss.

He hides along railway embankments,
in any scrubland
and strains to hear the train.
Vibrations coming nearer,
shoots to take cover between the steady roots
of an old, crinkled tree.

Quiet and shaky
he nervously grooms himself.
He sniffs obsessively
as it passes.
Beady eyes observe
speeding passengers
who do not return
his gaze.

Then all is restored.

Clouds blanket,
the sun dims, night wakes.
Woodland mouse emerges
in a frenzy of activity.
He pushes,
rolls,
heaves
dusty nuts, seedlings
and berries into his burrow.
Cosily at ease
away from prying eyes,
nibbles ferociously at his feast.

Moonshine

Celestial stars sprinkle like sugar,
I bob in the liquid night.
Mother Turtle beneath the sea
like a lump in my throat.
I know her anguish
I know what's in store.
Inertia of tears
swelling the tides,
they bulge and push
her faster towards the beach.
I understand,
I'm here with you.

Green Turtles have travelled
this passage for centuries,
laden with eggs
and a natural need.
Wading across coarse sand
to disperse their creamy bubbles,
their off-spring.

But extinction rests upon them
like a weighty shell,
I want to help
prevent the carnage.
I shine upon the Turtle, my daughter of the night.
She, the mother who is woebegone.
I light her path.
I shouldn't.
The poachers will follow
and rob her of her precious cargo.

They crouch there waiting
and I've seen it too many times.
I want to vanish
be snuffed out like a candle.
Where are the clouds?
Conceal me before it's too late!

The clouds do not come but the menace does,
with sacks agape
swallowing the Turtle's young.
A delicacy for some.

They shall not take all.
Some shall be spared to repeat the journey again.
Heavily swelling females will return
to these nesting beaches.
As if they have a choice!
They cannot stop the natural trend
and again, I shall hang my head helpless
and observe.

Poet Tree

Standing
tall and noble.

Shading
the fertile word.

Spreading
its thoughts wide.

Rooted
in hungry souls.

Safe With Me
– for Grandad

Ankle-deep in bluebells
I crushed a scent to remind me
of you
and all this
lifted, like the sweet dew
of my innocence.
I wish I could gather a mass of bells,
I would offer them to you.
I'd nestle in the dappled
shade, between streams of light
and harvest the waif hands
reaching out to me.

*

Treading behind,
pulling his cardigan
out of shape and heady with
simplicity. I wanted reassurance
behind his smile. He didn't mind me
talking incessantly
while we carelessly picked blackberries and
thorns. *All horses sleepwalk at dusk,*
we'll watch them one day.
The day consumed us.
Nodding blackberries turned into a mauve
haze, swaying in the heat
of my fond childhood.

*

Christmas ringlets and velvet
blue, I wore your smile
for you
while you struggled with consciousness
upon my front doorstep.
On tiptoes
to kiss and squeeze you goodbye,

I remember your hands
loose and shivering from shock.
We couldn't acutely comprehend
that April would loom, a mass of bells would bloom
but first the New Year would visit
without you.

School of Thought

Autumn afternoon, I feel
the silence cloak me.
On a step alone
I can visualise. Not noticeable

at first, caught in my own
state of mind, lines
lying across the grass. Hundreds
of lines
spun in the washing machine
spider. Eight legs walking
the tightrope. They dare

to bungee jump across
like monkeys, fearless in dense jungle.
It must have been
magical,
pupils observe with utmost interest,
caught in a trance
of wonder.

I shake it off and leave them
to their business, and sit drinking
the landscape.

Strait-lace

A hedge sits bathing in

intricate light

flimsy streams velvety

threads crossing webs

catching drops of dew.

Glittering and frail

like sequins.

Spider's needles

spin silk connecting the lacy

leaves. By dusk

the hedge is transformed.

Nature's veil heavy with a kiss.

Encompasses all.

The Gift

The Moon croons in the darkness,
she answers his call.
Still and secret.
Sigh-breaths of stars
caress the trees,
they wait and sparkle silvery
reflecting in her eyes.

Drops trickle down the rockface
to rest in shallow pools,
making her feel sad.
Voices vibrate through the current
and she knows them,
one drowns the rest
to tell her the Moon is waiting.

She is woven into the mystery of night.
Gazing down she sees
cupped in her hands
is the Moon.
Concentrating on his milky face,
she smiles.
The dense water seeps
through her fingers and the Moon melts,
but before he leaves
she wholly absorbs his spirit.

The Mistake

a cry wasting in her mouth
like flesh in the earth
remorse still thick
like blood of birth

soil rich red
burning bones of night air
virgin wolves straggle
like plunging thorns they stare

the Witches dance and circle
she still sheds no guilt
their revenge inevitable
her strength begins to wilt

suspicion breeds
the she-curse overcasts
kneeling in self-pity
the only light half mast

she pleads in vain
black enthusiasm used
Witches in blindness
scream out she is accused

they kiss the earth
worship their vanish from dawn
she who once knelt
left disfigured and torn

Tilled Earth

Her life now paler than wax.
Her dark smooth eyes watering
to look up at the sunburnt sky.
From tilled earth she rises
unashamed from her wooden cocoon,
the sun flutters down onto her shoulders
and she becomes eager to live, again.
As untamed as the wind,
to dance like a soft-thumbed leaf
in the jail of her keyless smile.
Windy-grey and barefoot;
sweet heather is stroked by her skin.
She glides without a sheet of sleep
in hushed movements of her irises,
salting the desolate moors
in a pool of words unaged, unheard.
Yearning for his soul.
Taunting him as clearly as her whisper.
Agonising both their minds.
Gold-tipped trees curtsey down in sympathy,
obeying every howl as she passes
like a thirsty stem stalking water.
Youth is lost,
yet **Death** is hers,
like a crow of laughter,
a shadow of love when she calls
and it flashes from her eyes,
bringing time to its knees
forever more.

Traditional Murderer

bulging eyes
dilated pupils
the smell of fear
emitting
from his pores
blood
pulsating
through
his body
foaming at
the mouth
heart
trembling
faster
breaths coming
in short gasps
no time
to think
nowhere
to hide
runs
until he
drops
gives up
accepts his fate
hounds catch up
savagely
bite
rip
tear him
from
limb to limb
within seconds
unrecognisable
the hunter
proudly holds
the bloody brush
high
symbol of sport
victory
in his eyes
satisfied
dressed
for the occasion
in red
and black
sickeningly
refined
a traditional
murderer

Undisturbed

As new spring has brought vivid
flowers and colour blooms,
hazy trees fill with flocks of song, warmth

and summer sanctuary. Autumn nibbles
at the trailing edge. Shadows
lengthen, evenings cool. Cloudy

and twirling winds twist through
the woods, birds gather moss and crumbly
leaves. Squirrels gorge themselves on nuts, berries

bloom red. The inhabitants prepare
for stretched winter, hibernate
as the silky snowflakes smother. Sleep.

Victory Song

Early morning high in tree
sings a chirpy robin.
His territory marked,
zealous redbreast suffers no intruders.
His chorus warns
other robins away.
If ignorance should wander
into another's province
a fly-chase would ensue.

*

The victor
perches proudly
on a prominent branch,
like an unmovable
Indian Brave
he sings
in high note
his song of Victory.

Windows

    I'm lost in looking
touch has no meaning.

    I'm positive a door is somewhere,
perhaps beneath the water.

    Where looking cannot wander
and seek out the window

    between fading mystery
and abstruse tomorrow.

    I'm too afraid to search
for what I seek,

    I will leave it to
the swimming wind.

    But even the wind
must remember

    windows can heal us one side
and haunt us the other.

Your Eyes
- for Sophie

Little windows to your heart.
The green tenderly soft,
gleams love and sadness
in the white specks that
attract my attention
like pinpointed stars.
You shine everything to me
in those eyes,
even the casted shadows
over my future.
The colour of grapes
with glowing warmth behind,
tearful
yet you never show it.
We shall when the time comes.
Until then I can drown
in your green sea, that in waves
of our friendship envelop me.

*

Regardless of what separates us
I know these tender moments
shall merge,
when I remember your eyes.

Midway Point

Absence

Loop by loop
the unique
delicate
daisy chain
of our beautiful friendship uncoils.
Without new memories to build upon
the stems dry, become brittle straw.

It started with the absence of you.
The absence of your kind words.
The absence of your support.
The absence of your crazy humour.
The absence of your fashion tips.
The absence of your knowing smile.
The absence of your birthday card
upon my mantelpiece.
Something you would never forget.

Amongst all the settled cowslips
I am but one small daisy,
waiting to be crushed
in the palm
of the hand
that life
dealt
it.

Acts

Act 1

I promised you
I would never take you for granted.
Do you remember
I guided you up the stairs,
winding
to the highest part
and how happy you were
in my hands?
Sat at the top, curled
into arms and legs
and heat.
A pair of homeless lovers
in our own temporary space
and the city
at our feet.

I had kept the key
and surprised you.
My reward -
an insistent, urgent,
virginal passion
of deep kisses
dragging me down
to my knees.
We were twelve stories up
when we found that blissful state
of stillness
and the blue lights
went out.

Act 2

A decade on
a union
a son
a home
and you complete me.
I overflow, you show
me new things
through your eyes and
I see why.
You have a way of letting me
know I am yours.
Have you told me lately? Yes, you have.

Balloons

A harsh month and the branches became needy.
Instead of fighting the wind, they used it.
The lonely twigs contorted into spindly webs until one night
they adopted two balloons.

One pink, one purple, they were heading towards the sea.
Puffed up and bold, slightly erratic until becoming ensnared.
They dangled and disco'd there bemused.
They entered into a pact -

one would not leave without the other.
The tree stood flamboyant, so different now in its row
with entertaining accessories for company. A few children pointed,
a few others noticed the twins.

Not one fireman came to rescue them. They writhed and struggled
with boredom. A captivating sadness. At night, I would watch the icy air
toy with their emotions. The balloons gave up their ghosts
and sighed

and sighed, until they shrunk into themselves.
Both became smaller
and smaller
until they were unrecognisable.
Like healthy grapes ripening into raisins.

Ceramic

Pottery in motion -
it flows, it's lucid
but it chips from time to time.
In a cold clump of clay
is the start of another one

and not one is the same.

They have flaws, dents,
charming disfigurements
from rushing, dancing
in circles.
Nurtured
between motherly hand
and forceful thumb
on a moist wheel.

The water sprinkles like fairy dust,
just in time
to tweak the mud
and gently, gently
turnabout,
ease it out
like a slippery
word
plummeting
purposefully
onto
paper.

Little clay poems in display cabinets
have cooled over the years.
Weathered ashy dust,
with the swift flick of a feather
from a sentimental duck.
Then read and re-read with certainty
and uncertainty.

Descriptive under glaze,
like slaves to the Poet's wheel
waiting steadily
to start turning
into enlightenment
once more.

Cross-stitches

You begin
face down
like a heavy black book
on knees.

A prayer
between hands
anchors
the Eve in you.

Mouth dry as wine
stalls your song
in church
this time.

Such
heavy hymns
open
tiny cross-stitches
of your past.

You lay out
on a slender pew,
to be a raft
and beam
anew.

Dock at your strong point
                        eventually.

Desir de l'Ange

C'etait son amour.
Her promise.
Her time.

*

Captured in a jewel of rain
her eyes peeping.
Glowing on the cliff-top
her figure appears,
locked in her heart
a flame of patience.
Hands gently holding
damaged sea shells,
she will follow
destitute footprints of the tide

in a dream
she cannot wake.
An entrapped mind
in a twinkle of forbidden hours,
sculpted in indigence
her silhouette spans the long days.
The sunset of her Memoirs
bloom across, filling le ciel.
A second set of footprints
encourages her to sea.
What is she searching for?

*

It was her history.
It was her fault.
Son coeur.

Favourite Sitting

A young Islamic girl takes sips of her first coffee.
From a second-storey window
five fashion torsos line up;
four paper females precede a male.
The pink-sequin flush of pigeons' necks
group over a fascination. A long-haired blonde
with a smoky cup
waits
for a rendezvous by his watch.
A muttering lady holds herself
in mirthful conversation,
while an elder sister treats
with a saucer of joy.
Smokers recline and enjoy the sight
of a man in swaying leather, they reach absentmindedly
for more ashtrays.
An Asian bicycle rider swerves amicably
around tight lovers. 'Imagine' plays
for the second time and a black and red photographer
crouches down; hunting
for his perfect angle.
A pair of old-timers stroll from the sunset, following
their ageless shadows toward supper.
And no one notices
the happy poet
writing like fire in the lit-up window of Starbucks.

Hope

It's like a game of hide and seek,
I close my eyes
then I find you.
I'm so glad I did,
we have a LOT of catching up to do!
Up to old tricks,
the old me,
we're neither in a yesterday or today.
It's the feelings that matter
the most.
Reunited, the duo, unstoppable!
Safe.
My heart expands,
begins to believe again,
a goofy grin all over my face

then I wake
into this breathing vessel
and remember.
It's still the aching, parting, deepening chasm.
Why does the mind act so cruel? Play stupid tricks?
Hope is not a game
after all.

How It Must Be

The sleeves of trees
drop their leaves,
they curl like wreaths
beneath your feet
and huddle in packs
against railway tracks,
finding warmth in numbers.
Whilst parent trees slumber,
the tingle of their future
dawns on them.

When not watched,
they explore
all the more
darting passed your lids,
flocking like birds,
skimming the ocean,
shrugging off the notion
of being contained
within the family frame.

They will find a home
that suits them best.
Maybe
quietly against a grave
or nurtured into a nest;
and all their springs and summers
easily forgotten
with the rest.
Youth becomes the unreachable dream
that once fed the tree.

I wish

that we didn't know
what we know.

That we didn't understand
what we understand.

Life
would be so much easier
that way.

J Shed

on that first night
frost-curves against the skylight
echoed the January crescent
peeping
coyly
as she let her guard down
as she clambered to sleep

*

on that first morning
feet
  pattered
down
     in a
 spiral
    to
tentatively
stop upon a step
she exhaled
took in a new view
realised
she was finally on her first

Life in a Cemetery

Modest dreamers carve
into a humble unspoiled plain, a refuge.

Upon a defaced grave, a blue-tit chirps,
blossom envelops the dead with borrowed thyme.

Valerian clambers heartily
across the bones of the Church and ivy leaves

drape over sunny sides of tombstones.
Ferns spread between families.

Lichens unfold like maps
and a cat stretches her paws, keeping watch

from the high railings.
A protective ambience blankets

the soil, which is acidy and restful.
Until daffodils play in harmony,

to awaken other striking flowers and stir
lazy bees to present themselves.

All of life's sweet nectar dearly
reminding us

our stories never stand alone,
nature's soft wing beats against them.

Meaning

adrift under
freckled stars
heart beating softly
to darkened grace
midnight swims
in guilt
crushed dust
foolishly dominant
steals a glint
wading its way
to the rest
curving into
one another
like harp strings
beckoning an
intense view
sailing in a
private torture
balancing
on impulse
stirring close
like thunder
a shining moment
a phenomenon

November

flame and brimstone
whooshed up to match
the expectant stars
like fast sparks
when our eyes met
and
we felt it
too

two
half-full mugs of coffee
held sweet
moments of acquaintance
in every sip
because we were more
engrossed in our
beginning

too
intrigued to notice
your watch had spun
past the curfew
and we clung to each other's
memories
upon leaving
that first embrace
at the call
of a sharp whistle

Quiet

words skirl in the past
but it is still dark there
for me
for
you, will not say
will not bless my ear

how many times
did you
blink your eyes?
as many
as your tap-dancing heartbeats?
your lines weren't set deep enough
for all the laughter you had left
to laugh

of all the sitting time spent
in an overcast soul search
searching
for me
sans
you, would not say
would not bless my ear

each move of the hand is profound
and thrusts me
further
from us
how powerful a force
time is

Salisbury Eve

Time stands beside you
From mist and sun
You are crowned
Harmonising the clouds
I will not falter
As I balance
Upon the sight of you
I find no comparison
To your archway of light
And softness of stone
A peacefulness from your slim windows
Spans across blessed grass
Your history is seen
In the heart of the street
Beyond rhythmic branches
To clay in clear water
And dedicated benches
I am home in a vision
And the journey never tires
I prickle in anticipation
I feel so small
A calm breath in
A thought returns to my lips
Reading my smile
I remember our past
And the spell that you cast
It is enough to just be
You are young to me

Tealight

Two little tealights side by side,
lit up and happy
until one of the flames faltered
and died,
then a loving hand
cupped around
the remaining tealight,
as if to say -
*Although things won't be the same
lonely tealight,
your fire will burn twice as bright*

*in memory
of his name.*

Thirty-one

If
I could
put into words
how short your life
spanned, I think people would
be truly shocked to visually understand,
each one of these words represent how long
you had.

Thistle and Twilight

So, it is laid to rest.
These tired lips
hush the dawn of you.
Bereft like a thistle in my room
without water.

... softest water
and travelling pictures
shrouded in a castle turret;
to the secret gates
of named Saints
and the wheel of light.

Steeply down
as twilight crowns
the far-off Arthur's Seat,
its special place
looming equal to her hand.

The smell of winter
and a quick squirrel
grey as the cobbled hills,
home to the grand old Banks
lit up in a grand circle.

One cassette on repeat
weaving between
the tallest of the tall.
Her impressed face
behind a car window,
staring at
snowfall.

Surreal memories
imprint
on my mind
but then the engine takes a breath...

and unwaveringly
I trail off
like a single note of music.

No longer in that dream
… of the train between
the craggy mountains,
all wearing beards of mist.

The wonder is left behind,
back to my tired lips
that hush
the dawn
of you.

Tresses

An accessory like no other.

A bedhead of halo-shine wanton of attention, a diva.

Devoted lashings of locks, soft as a lamb's curl.

Righteously sitting like a conscience on shoulders.

Voluminous pride not unlike the beating bounce of a lion's mane, in captivating slow motion.

An extension of feelings pulling the whole look together. Effortlessly.

Curvaceous enough to heart-frame my face. Beguiling enough to turn heads. Thick enough to
smother my pillow. Dear enough to be considered friend.

Oh! How I have missed you!

Vienna to London 1936
- for Olive

I could not snuff out the sweet luxury
my heart so rekindled.
And to leave Vienna
brought a pearl to my eye, a luminescent sigh
as the Express rolled in.

But then, a chance encounter!
The compressed compartment
must still contain our secrets, low murmurs strumming
against strings of the window. All night
he spoke to me.

Coffee refreshed my senses.
I mounted the Dover Ferry
full of surprises, still glad of his company.
Tilting to listen and smiling to please, the scent of his suit
on the sea breeze.

Captivating conversations
overtook the slow train to London. To other eyes
we looked like fate. Sparkling,
playful banter over a cloth-strewn table, the plan
was set.

Reluctantly
we parted ways on an angled street.
Such long goodbyes, a kiss or two
in the air. Hoped again we would meet,
but knew it wouldn't be fair.

*

To this day I have kept you.
Precious, private, etched in a box.
Your charm - beats faster when I catch myself
journeying back
to the preordained seat, you so kindly offered.

Words

The simplest thought
giving itself
in marriage
to paper.
A kind of sharing.
Intimate
literature.
It has stolen you.

You Took Flight
- in memory of Richard Peel, my best friend.

Your well-loved words
cannot bring your voice to me;
which only last week rang so clear.
How did you used to sound?
No honest answer can be found.
Please laugh aloud with me, bend in two.

My dreams are uneasy
as I search for your face,
a familiar expression,
the way your mouth would curve
into the funniest of smiles.
Over the top drama and
your Hollywood mannerisms
are so poignant to every boxed memory.

I keep thinking of birds when I think of you.
Their flight, their freedom, their peace.
Symbols of comfort,
making me glad
to have safely stowed similar
trinkets and canvasses,
in the nest of my rooms.

One bird hanging from a ribbon
of grey,
completes my classic look.
I just know you would approve
albeit for the occasion.
Will it bring me peace to feel closure?
Will the simple warmth of a gathering crowd
help me feel less lonely?
I will try to keep my promise.

Why is fragility
a part
of a person,
of life,

an organ,
a breath?
You have opened up
so many questions.

It perplexes me
that I shall never see you old.
Our last cinema trip replays in my mind
bittersweetly.
Two pensioners in the front row
might once have been us
but only I know,
we will never be them.

My heart
conspires against me
like a heavy, paperweight sigh.
Yearning
over and over.
I miss you
over and over,
again.
A testament true
to how rich
you made every day.

Thank you
for diminishing a little of the fear
of my ultimate The End.
True to your way,
always looking after me
like a bodyguard, remember?
Thank you too
for quoting A Cup of Sun,
you always knew
the right thing to say.
You quoted *a bird doesn't sing because it has an answer,*
it sings because it has a song.

You had a song too
and it was very, very beautiful.

The Other Day

1853 - 1890

I collect your memories
in Zundert
like a child following
a Flower Parade,
consuming the last
sunny rays of kindness
in their pockets.

I collect your thoughts
in the quiet hours
when brushwork hushes
your lips
to conformity,
like a tight bud yielding
to the sun.

I collect you
from the back door
of The Yellow House,
where you start to unfold
in the brass sunlight,
bubble-born
of flame, and leaves
of your aesthetic history spread
like the wildest sunflower.

1926 - 1962

I collect your images
projected
as a Vogue bombshell; demure
in a last sitting.
But so suggestive in the past
like an easy lover pin up, hot
round lips pressed
to the glass.

I collect your feelings
split
like a grenade,
coquettishly
grossly misunderstood.
Pining for a maternal
script
in a fame-induced scene.

I collect you
after month six
in Brentwood, an oasis
of eerie calm
implodes. Everyone realises
they didn't know you
well enough to save you.
Dramatically,
tragically, you turn over the newest leaf,
you have completed your journey.

Best. Day. Ever.

A man made of twilight haunts Swansea marina. While courting
over blue bridges we pass many times. We don't know him
by name, we recognise his freshness, his booming Hello as bold and clear
as a ship's bell.
A button; fastening us in simple courtesy.

This quotidian routine brings great purpose and his welfare
becomes part of our familial strolls, always generating friendly waves
and Hello there's to one and all and
although it's not the norm, we bob at his quirkiness.

A day comes,
when the sail bridge buckles under weight of people dolloped in one place, overspilling
his route. The joy he utters meets a plethora
of interesting faces escaping a conference, idly ambling.
He receives them all like celebrities.

Whether in pairs, groups or a sloop like him. Not one breath-pause.
Echo-bellows Hello. Hello. Hello there!
gratefully receiving hundreds back until we guess he floats home, vocally exhausted.
Giggling, we imagine he'll scope out a stadium or theatre to visit next.

BFF

Oh! What times we had!
Countless times
taking on that steep Tumble hill
to reach campervan sleepovers
and Dirty Dancing.
I remember you came late to school
and were drawn to me, immediately
like a magnet.
We'd crimp our hair
and wear matching dungarees,
sing out of tune to Mariah Carey.
We could quote every word
that Belle said
and we had similar crushes.
You were a dark-haired Cameron Diaz
to my swotty Julia Roberts,
and I remember plenty of microwave meals
babysitting and Sound of Music.
Lots of Rimmel swaps and pouty lips,
shrimps for you
fried eggs for me.
We'd swing on swings
and agree on things,
especially that Bon Jovi was dreamy.
We shared hurts and pains
were going to run away
but went to see Macbeth in Aberystwyth!
Nothing could phase us.
We were the sisters we never had.
After exams, we split down the middle
I went to Sixth Form
you went to Birmingham
and eventually we lost touch.

But

I always wondered about you
until one day I found you
in a place I'd already been
countless times.
Exchanged numbers
met for coffee
and sat opposite
retelling stories
but our memories
weren't matching up.
I was happy for you.
You were married
had been a while
four kids
and a Bakery role.
I was engaged
the sparkle still new
personally assisting
and trying for a baby.
You had an adult
best friend
I'd cruelly lost mine
a year ago.
You were already set
in your ways
I wasn't in the same mould.
I was fighting against it
but it felt like
you and I had been reduced
to simple acquaintances.
There was no easy way
to say it.
What happened to us?
Nothing major,
just time.

Clove Hitch Knot

It's natural I should worry how they will be received
I am only human.
They will be laid bare in a vulnerable state
for easy consumption,
pored over
intellectually, critically.
All the innermost subdivisions
unraveled

like a knot hitch clove.

Please let them be
discovered on a good day.
Don't let them be wholly understood so eager winds
may rush through reasons
to try again.
I just need a sign-divine the masses crave more.
One knee down, until the starting pistol shoots
me weaving into airy thought into typed tale,
cutting, styling, repeat.

Gwendraeth

the important place
where I attempted my first forward roll, downed turkey burgers and
hot chocolate

lived in the library
was an Adoring Girl, cooked my first jacket potato, played Lily Moffat

in The Corn is Green
asked Hilary Llewellyn-Williams for feedback, read Cosmopolitan,
did pass Geography

listened to Toni Braxton
on shared earphones, stopped a real-life scrap, earnt my 10-metre
swimming badge

saved an injured blackbird
witnessed Ouija boards, was obsessed with badminton, made
Eisteddfod flower girl

voted for the first time.
I was so much more than just a keen student I was part of
something rarely seen

that shaped me solid
as I am today, in my gratefulness I Googled to show my son where I
went as a girl

but you were sealed tight
no longer in use, forgotten on detention. A Grammar School once,
not a second word

I was left speechless

In a Marriage

Ceremony, I placed the ring
upon your wrong finger
and you laughed
with me
then.

Now,
I realise
the ring isn't
on the right person
you won't hurt me again.

Labour of Love

We don't have time
to love each other
the way we did
before

you. Never ever
felt this utterly
exhausted before
we'd

call it a night.
Something
has to give
if our toothbrushes
touch

more in their pot
than we
do
in bed.

Like it's 1998

Take a trip with me   down memory lane   to College Street   Salisbury   a second-storey bedroom   a friendly tree   a room-mate fish   too many candles   crunchy nut cornflakes   mugs of tea   a galley kitchen   Lighthouse Family   All Saints   Alanis Morrisette   Uninvited   Iris   City of Angels   Meg Ryan and Nicolas Cage   two flings   a long-distance relationship   first salon haircut   second ear piercing   plait   wedges   trouser skirt   an anklet   in Casa Fina   to the cloisters   Magna Carta   the tallest spire   alone in the city   sketching elephants   sitting under a willow tree   solo Sunday cinema trips   Meet Joe Black   Saving Private Ryan   Practical Magic   long   luxurious   baths   one   epic thunderstorm   Bodyshop   Dewberry   raspberry   shampoo   an   orb on the staircase   a 'fall' down the stairs   big bag of pink lady's   a market chant   a pretty flower for a pretty face   finding Waitrose   La Senza   Bay Trading   MVC   Woolworths   Blockbuster   Titanic on video   Doritos to go   Cheungs Chinese   La Gondala   putting electricity on a key   Witches coven   night trips to Wales   veggie pate   playing Spirit in The Sky   Monday mornings   early photocopying   a dial-up modem databases   ducks   orange juice   window watching   Doorstep sarnies   Hideous   Kinky   Star   Wars   ticket   for   a   homeless   man   Odeon   Pick n Mix   Reeves Bakery   cheese twists   cappuccino doughnuts   conferencing   at   Loughborough   Uni   a   Nottingham stop   day-trip to Shaftesbury   another to Bath   back to my favourite bench   far right of the Cathedral   eating grapes from Sainsbury's   a best before date in 1998.

Mother, How Was I Made?

Your father and I congregated in a dark, warm corner.
Undisturbed; we fabricated you from hair, lint, dead skin, spider webs, light rubbish,

dust and debris.
Gradually over time
with incredibly slow movements,
you were shaped lovingly
into the ball of life you are today.
You are held together by static electricity,
unseen by the human eye.
And if you hopped (like our namesake)
you would fall apart, my love.
So, you must stay in this warm corner
and studiously practice a complete lack of movement
or change. Preserve your textured self
in flecks of mind
like a drowsy bijou Buddha. You are a young shepherd
tucked in the nape of the mountain.

In time, you will naturally grow in size as more lint,
dust and debris flock to you. But for now, rest your wide eyes,
explore inner sparks.

NY

I take my time
and glimpse at living
faces, height makes them
speckle the glass. Each one an
individual tiny world of familiarity

but one face
holds my gaze longer,
like patience. Clenching my
questions and running through
answers, breathing low on street blocks.

I wait curiously.
Alone and compressed
by boxed air, in every vision
goes a second. The truth sometimes
disappoints my reality, where siren sounds

evaporate,
like colours leaving
seasonal patterns in my docile
mind. Until thunderclaps are flying and
all I think about is how can I reach, reach, reach?

Oestrogen

A woman
runs
out of this
like a car
runs out
of petrol.

But unlike
a car
a woman
cannot
simply
refuel.

Peeling Mushrooms
- for Will

I remove jewellery
You pause your game
We stand side by side
Little and large
Twelve cups before us
We peel softly
We speak simply
Engrossed in an unpaid chore
Yet one we can afford to enjoy
In our happy place
At the start of a meal
Behind the scenes
Our lines in sync
Making a modest pile
I go to the fridge
Source a block of cheese
You tell me all about
Blocks and wither storms
We chuckle
At all the small stuff
That happened today
While our knuckles
Graze the cushion-domes
Of turtle shells
So many have turned over
And you've beaten me again
Because I let you

Positive

Positive Dysphotopsia, it sounds like an alien utopia
and the reason for its existence is equally as sci-fi - the YAG laser.
It was meant to eradicate posterior capsular opacification
but that remains to be seen.

The probe 'gifted' me the ability to see
a windscreen wiper of intense light, blading and sweeping across
my sight from left to right like the membrane blink
of a Whiptail Lizard.

If this were a rare occurrence, it would be beautiful
such as a phenomenon unexplained.
But it's like a parasite taking up room in my vision; and it's so well hidden;
not even with their technology and great advances, do Optometrists see it.

There is no visible way to reverse this,
I have to use mind control, neuroadaptation to breeze through the day.
Except it's not so easy in summer, when modest sunbeams
ignite their solar and flare across my eye.

And though it doesn't hurt, the constant aura magnifies
when I realise it will never leave my left eye. It's here for the long haul.
I commend anyone who finds themselves in this pickle,
because ironically, it's hard to remain optimist in such bright times.

Stella

You'd have to wait a lengthy month
before seeing me again.
To have someone else to talk to
besides Moira Stuart.

You were a retired nurse, a widow,
at your window
with curlers in, the hob on
and an electrifying sense of purpose.

I was a young student
on a mission to bring library books,
all very local,
I volunteered my time away.

I had plenty to give
and you craved that contact.
Our friendship flourished out
of you being a young me and I being an old you.

And the older I get
I can see the appeal.
I was sweet sixteen, literally on the cusp
and you wanted to share that with me.

If only I could tell you
all the things that have happened
since then, you'd drop your Welsh cake!
I have so many revelations to reveal.

Stella,
I just wanted to say
that oftentimes I think of you.

I am ashamed to admit
I can't recall all we talked about,
but I have a feeling you clung
to every word.

The Poetess' Husband
- for John

She perches snuggly on a mossy chair,
spins on five brass wheels branching out.
Attached amusingly to a much-used pencil
lightly raps the wooden head of its aqua bunny
on her chin.
She thinks ...
peers out the window but all she ever sees
is the next sentence ahead.
Tilts her head, beams like a touch lamp.
Something of worth is imprisoned
and she means to unlock it by pounding keys.

*

Outstretched on the burgundy 'L' piece he knows
she's upstairs. Can hear her quietly thinking
and knows her birdish heart is answering the wild
vines that bind her. Attuned to her plight
he thinks ...
*I don't dabble
in this sorcery, but if it's something she loves
I will willingly love her for it.* Written all over her face
is her trembling voice reading aloud.
He is the science of reason, a warm balm, her defence
against doubtful squalls, the irreplaceable Poetess' Husband.

The Same

It was Tuesday, nothing remarkable except for a beautiful start.
Setting up in the Solicitor's office an aroma of fresh brews, buttery
bacon, found me. I spoke to former coal miners, compensating as I
ploughed through generous conversation, lots of staying on the
line. Especially to widows, who'd bring sweet biscuit-boxes at the
end. Amid emphysema, it wasn't unusual for men to wheeze
strange things. That afternoon *All hell's breaking loose in America!
It's World War 3!*

I recall thinking *bless, he must be watching an old war movie.*
Yet something in his tone stayed salient around my shoulders. I
underplayed with the girls but one suggested tuning in and dug out
a huge chunk of radio, to be afflicted by one broadcast on every channel -
the same Towers had been hit. New York was collapsing and her citizens
unrecognisable. Numb, briefcase carrying, ash-
smoke stumbling apparitions. When plumes cleared neither were
left standing. A piano note pierced hearts. All of us fell silent, icons
un-twinned, history cemented.

Trolls

In the 59th year of the 19th century there lived a ravenous troll
under a dank Norwegian bridge.

Now 20th Century Studios explode our screens with singing trolls
under reams of skittle-candy pixels.

But my favourite trolls were created
under a Russ label with clone faces, protruding bellies and always a
good hair day.

I had a Mexican one in a poncho
     Hawaiian one in a grass skirt
          bunch of keyring ones with florescent hair
               and a handful of minis with scented hair.

They were easily the best sort of Christmas presents I coveted, and
I think I need more!
Maybe I'll find flame-haired fun hiding in the copious land of eBay.

Unexpected Visitor

How inappropriate a time

to call round, I must say!

It's only 5am.

I'm cleaning my teeth.

I'm on the school run.

I'm in a meeting.

I'm still on the bus.

I'm running a bath.

I just don't have time

to write, right now.

But I will cling to what you said,

I will pop the kettle on,

I will get my head down

and I will do you justice.

We Dared to Dance in Odeon

Enchanted credits rolled, we liked to stay till the end

of films which spoke to us. Quoting back lines, voicing

Blunt, Hathaway, Adams, Danes, Pfeifer, Streep, geeky

I know! Worries? - they'd popped into thin air like puffy kernels

salty to sweet. Just two award winning crazies! At the arc of our row

you held out your hand, I joined in dancing lavishly free. In this memory,

we will always be a pair of synonyms pirouetting, revolving

around each other.

*

Yvaine - *'What do stars do? Shine.'*

You are here

at last
after ten, twenty, thirty years
meditating in Brusali.
Always a constant.
Giving counsel
and release.

                                        No control
                            over where and when
                                  I might write.
                              Ebbing in and out,
                                        so, I go
                                  with the flow
                         if no pen, draft a text.

The thought
has played on my mind
a few times.
Procrastinating very personally,
very unsure
the rework
is right.

                                    A collective
                                  of old friends
                            who know me so well.
                            A little ray of light,
                                  when I lift
                                  up the screen.

The everyday
a hustle and bustle
and becoming a Mama,
the best distraction
of all.
While you brewed
a little longer.

Then.
This year.
This month.
I marched on working
from home,
mundanely tapping away.
When finally something
clicked!

www.ingramcontent.com/pod-product-compliance
Lightning Source LLC
Chambersburg PA
CBHW041309110526
44590CB00028B/4300